Table Tennis

D0531346

John Hilton

Table Tennis

With Richard Eaton of the
Sunday Times

Stanley Paul
London Melbourne Sydney Auckland Johannesburg

Acknowledgement is due to the help of Mary Eaton, Rose D'Sa and Sue Ashton, without whom this book could not have been completed.

Stanley Paul & Co. Ltd
An imprint of the Hutchinson Publishing Group
17–21 Conway Street, London W1P 6JD
Hutchinson Publishing Group (Australia) Pty Ltd
PO Box 496, 16–22 Church Street, Hawthorne, Melbourne, Victoria 3122
PO Box 151, Broadway, New South Wales 2007
Hutchinson Group (NZ) Ltd
32–34 View Road, PO Box 40–086, Glenfield, Auckland 10
Hutchinson Group (SA) Pty Ltd
PO Box 337, Bergvlei 2012, South Africa
First published 1985
© John Hilton and Richard Eaton 1985
Illustrations © Stanley Paul & Co. Ltd 1985
Set in Linotron Plantin and Rockwell by
Wyvern Typesetting Limited, Bristol
Printed and bound in Great Britain by Anchor Brendon Ltd, Tiptree, Essex

ISBN 0 09 153631 6

Contents

Preface

John Hilton's achievement in winning the 1980 European title in Berne was one of the truly great sporting stories. He had not even begun to play the game full time. He was already thirty-two years old. And he was only number three in England. Yet he beat a whole series of leading men – Wilfried Lieck of West Germany, Gabor Gergely of Hungary, Jacques Secretin of France, and Josef Dvoracek of Czechoslovakia – to become the first Englishman ever to win the title. It was the equivalent of Bradford winning the FA Cup. Later, when finishing fifth in the World Cup, he showed he had also gained promotion to the table tennis equivalent of the first division.

Table tennis had never made the front pages of Fleet Street before, and generally the press made a great deal out of the almost unknown insurance salesman who made fools of some of the greatest players in the world. In some of the reports though there were hints of reservation. 'Funny bat', 'secret weapon', and even 'black bat out of hell' were some of the labels used to describe John's celebrated combination bat. This had one slow rubber plus a conventional faster one which he twirled and twiddled and with which he attacked and defended in so many variations of spins and tactics that nobody knew what he was going to do next.

Nobody was sure either just how much of his remarkable achievement was due to his great skill and ingenuity and how much to the bat. All that can be said for certain is that John had to learn two versions of every shot before he could use it. Then he had to put them all together in sequences in rally after rally without mistakes before he could win. This was another, different, equally remarkable achievement because it altered the way table tennis was played. Afterwards a bevy of players, many of them young ones, started developing combination bat styles and sequences. Since then the rules of table tennis have been changed. Different colours for each side have become obligatory.

The history-making ploy of putting dead anti-spin or anti-loop rubber on one side and a more conventional rubber on the other, and then twiddling, actually began far away on the other side of the world. The Chinese had become well known for twiddling on serve. Then one of the game's most independent and irreverent characters, Paul Pinkewich, many times Australian champion, returned home from Japan with some new rubbers. This was just at the time that John, who had emigrated to Australia for two years, fortunately decided that England, after all, was for him. He returned with the new materials to Manchester, and for months on end turned his spare room into a kind of table-tennis laboratory, experimenting with every kind of slow and fast rubber in every possible combination. Frequently this caused him to lose matches he might have otherwise won. He never stopped experimenting even when he had passed the age when table-tennis players are supposed to lose their reflexes and slow up. To learn how to play effectively with the best combination of rubbers took him altogether about five years.

Nobody should attempt quite the same thing today. The point about the story is that John's achievements reveal the daring, determination, dedication, imagination, analytical acumen, physical fitness, level-headedness and sheer courage that a person can discover in himself or herself – if he or she only digs deep enough for those resources. Of all the persons in England to whom the chance of winning a European title might have fallen John Hilton was the least likely to pass it up.

Nobody should attempt the same thing in quite the same way for two reasons. Firstly it is usually more important, when learning, to concentrate on your own technique – as those competing with normal reversed pimpled rubber do – rather than on the technique of other players and how to counter it, as combination-bat players tend to do. Secondly, such players are likely in future to be successful in fewer numbers now that the two-colour rule has been introduced. So beware. You are unlikely to be able to copy exactly what John Hilton did.

At the same time, combination bats, especially those with long pimples on one side, will probably still be around for some time. There is no harm in a player who already has good all-round stroke production trying to develop a special style with such equipment. The danger is for a young player beginning to rely on it before he has a good basic technique. Otherwise, combination bats may be fun and at the very least help to increase your knowledge of rubbers and spins. Some players may still prove to be effective with them. For these reasons an insight into their mysteries is provided in the pages of this book.

Richard Eaton
The *Sunday Times*

Introduction

Once you have developed your game it is very difficult to introduce new shots. They have to come first, and to acquire the complete game before bad habits set in the quicker the learning process the better. The oldest, one of the best, and frequently the quickest form of learning is imitation. Looking at the photograph flicker sequences in this book will give you the moving image of a shot necessary for that. The words that go with the sequences will help you to recognize and evaluate what you see, and sometimes to supplement it.

When you are trying to acquire a shot the secret is to practise it first but only to use it now and again when you play. Only gradually will you build it into your game. That is partly because practice and competition are two different things. (In a way it requires you to learn the shot twice – or at least to learn the same shot in two totally different situations.) It is also partly because your opponent may very well return your newly developed shot, and then you need to know how to follow it up. If, for instance, you learn how to play a good fast topspin but your recovery is slow and your blocking is bad, then your new shot will only land you in more trouble than if you had not used it. Many players learn how to develop a shot, or several of them, but improvement only comes from putting them together in sequences. You must build a complete game.

A beginner will often start by playing a bit of a forehand. With this you can cover much of the table, but as early as possible you need to play both a backhand and a forehand. That will in turn create the need to move bat, body and feet together. Too often you see coaches standing and hitting to a fixed place from a fixed position, and that can be fatal. You never get a ball like that in a match. As soon as you can hit a ball at all you should never be standing to play a shot. Playing a shot and moving to the next should be all one movement.

Developing technique is not the only important thing – so is the right mental approach. Sometimes too much store is placed on winning matches when players are young. A career lasts about ten to fifteen years as a senior, but probably less than half that time as a junior. Not till a player is in his mid-twenties, and possibly even later, will he or she be fully developed. Better to work towards that and not worry so much about results at junior level – provided you are working along the right lines. That means you have to go on developing all the shots, and also learning how to use them. Sometimes you may go backwards a little before going forwards again. It can take time. It also means being critical about what you do. It should be understood that this book is only one interpretation of the methods available in producing the many varieties of table-tennis shots. There are no rights or wrongs; the criterion by which a shot should be judged is its level of success, and the recovery required to play the next shot. Hopefully the following chapters will help you do this.

NOTE

Flicker pictures referred to in the text are identified by the sequence letter followed by the relevant page number; thus, the picture from sequence C on page 44 would be described as C44.

Chapter 1
Equipment

Equipment is of the first importance, particularly your bat. Bats come in different speeds, with different rubbers and sponges, and the choice is wide. Table tennis is one of the least expensive of all sports, but a bat will not be a cheap item if you make mistakes with your early purchases.

Coaches tend to say to beginners that they should buy a bat with control, a slow bat, which makes it easier to obtain feeling. In some ways it is better to go against that advice, and to choose a fairly quick rubber and a quickish blade. That way you will be using a bat suitable for play at a high level. If you start by playing the correct shots at speed, then you are accepting straight away how the game is to be played, and how you should try to develop. When players rally at a slower speed they can become mentally conditioned to this, which influences their technique. It is important to start playing and reacting in the way that makes you aware of the pace at which you must play if you are to be successful.

For maximum speed use a 2.5 mm sponge and for maximum spin, 1.5 mm rubber surface. The maximum permitted by the rules on one side of the bat is 4 mm with sponge and rubber together. More control is obtained by limiting the amount of sponge on the blade. Defensive players may play with only 1 mm which gives a lot of control but not much speed or spin. Over-the-

table players would normally use 1.5 or 2 mm and very fast topspin players would use 2.5 mm. Most top players use 2 to 2.5 mm of sponge. These days many players put bicycle glue (vulcanizing fluid) between the sponge and the rubber, not just as an adhesive, but because that also makes the bat faster.

What rubbers should you use?

There are a vast number of different rubbers – but you have to use those on the ITTF approved list. The great variety has helped develop a whole range of different styles of playing table tennis, probably more styles than in any other sport. You will have to choose something suitable for your style. It may be long pimples, short pimples, reversed rubber, dead anti-spin rubber, or possibly a combination bat with different rubbers on each side, but experiment and learn and take advice if necessary.

Most world-class players that use long pimples use them to defend, although occasionally – Carl Prean has been one – to block. If so, it has to be a flat block, not a topspin block. Anti-spin or anti-loop rubber, as it suggests, kills spin, and is slow, giving control. The fast, topspin rubber is the reversed 'normal' rubber. It is players who use this who most consistently come out on top, and should continue to do so because the game is only likely to get quicker.

To start with it is best to use the same rubbers on each side of the bat until you have developed a good technique. Reversed rubber, that is with pimples inwards against the sponge and a smooth surface, is the most common. You can progress to a combination bat later, if need be.

What blades should you use?

There are wood or carbon-fibre blades, but wood is probably better as carbon-fibre can be hard to control. Most players keep the same wood bat for the whole of their career. But they change their rubbers often. Once the rubber has gone dead and lost its feeling, and the surface no longer gets the grip or the spin, then the sponge with the rubber is removed and replaced. You should do the same. Change rubbers every few weeks if necessary, but get a blade you like and stick with it.

There are three kinds of blade: fast, made of seven-ply wood; medium, or a round blade as it is sometimes called, which is five-ply and gives control and speed together; and three-ply, which

most defensive players use, and which gives most control. The size of the blade is not too important. Nor is the shape.

You usually get used to the feeling of the weight of the rubber on the wood quite quickly. You can also get used to a heavy or light bat. But your ability to do so depends on what you use when you first begin. It may be best to start with a heavyish blade because that provides speed. There are two advantages to this: you can control spin with a heavy blade and you can give a lot of speed and spin. The heavier blade is normally a bit bigger so you may also have the advantage of a little more bat to play with.

You also need proper clothing – shorts or skirt and shirt that are dark, and good quality shoes. The shoes you use in competition are not to be recommended for training. For competition use a stronger shoe, neither a jogging shoe nor an outdoor shoe, but something in between with a bit of strength underneath. Over the years the constant pressure on ankles and knees means, unless they are supported, they may give you trouble later in your career.

Chapter 2
The Grip

SEQUENCE A
Backhand push

A bad grip will limit you throughout your career because once developed it is very difficult to adjust. And these limits are very restricting because to a large extent the grip influences the whole stroke.

You should shake hands with the bat, but don't go right up on the blade, and don't choke on it. Go too far up and you will lose flexibility in the wrist. Go too low and you have flexibility but you risk losing control. So hold it somewhere about the middle where you are not choking the shot, and the grip is relaxed enough to permit wrist control (see photographs 2 and 3).

SEQUENCE B
Forehand loop

You should be able to see a small gap between the middle finger and the end of the blade. If you hold it higher up, some part of the inside of that finger and the hand is in contact with the blade. Away from the blade the middle finger is more flexible and you have more relaxation.

Sometimes top players, such as Istvan Jonyer of Hungary, drop the hand down the handle during the rally. He might do it playing away from the table when he needs to hit the ball with a little more strength. He has a good body action so the wrist and the bat are just an extension of himself. But he is a special player who has developed this over the years. It is not to be advised for beginners, or even for most of the advanced players.

SEQUENCE C
Backhand sidespin
serve

Some players use one grip for the backhand and alter it for the forehand. They move the bat in the palm of the hand using thumb and forefinger. But to develop all the strokes properly you should keep one grip because it makes control easier.

SEQUENCE D
Backhand chop

13

1

2

3

The penholder grip, mostly used by Asian players, has the handle in an upright position and you hold it as if you were holding chopsticks (see photograph Jiang Jia-liang of China, the 1984 World Cup winner on page 15). The advantage is that it is not necessary to turn the bat round for backhand and forehand – you use the same side. But more Chinese players use the shakehands grip, or Western grip, these days than they used to.

The penholder is often very good for blocking because you can get right above the ball, and also obtain a better angle. With the Western grip the bat is to the side of the wrist when you block, whereas with the penholder the wrist is above. The penholder is also good for serving because of the spin the wrist above the bat can get.

Chapter 3
Service

A good service is immediately useful. One half of a table tennis match gives you the chance to take the initiative straight away. There are many types of serve, and the more you use, the better the chance of gaining the initiative. Take for instance one of the most common, a backhand spin serve which may look the same each time but can be delivered with several varieties of spins. The opponent can then be kept permanently guessing. There are three main types – sidespin, chop and float.

For the sidespin serve, the stance will often be fairly sideways although you can see from the flicker sequence that this is not necessarily so. Normally you should have the weight on the front foot, which is the right foot (photograph 5), and you would generate more sidespin the further across that foot is. But if you want to put more backspin on the ball you can do so better with the weight on the left foot. You chop (or backspin) the ball more easily when you are facing straight down the table. Some serves of course are combinations of the two. If you stand square it is difficult to get sidespin but what Hungary's Tibor Klampar, the former World Cup winner, does is a semi-spin serve. Sometimes there is little or nothing on it, sometimes it is a sidespin and sometimes a chop.

There tends not to be a vast distinction between these serves, because Klampar doesn't want to put too much spin on the ball and in this way he ensures the return will be less spinny. He wants the return to be flicked rather than pushed with back-spin. A serve with no spin also makes it very difficult to return the ball short and low. Klampar can then easily follow up with his topspin. Klampar will also serve short and tight so that the receiver cannot topspin, and if he does flick it will not carry much spin.

16

4

How to stand

To do these serves you would stand over towards
the backhand corner (see photograph C15 of the
flicker sequence). For the backspin or chop serve,
take the blade of the bat slightly more under the
ball. With the sidespin, pull the bat across the back
and inside the ball more. The follow-through across
the body (picture C75) makes you ready to play a
forehand loop (picture C91). You can also add further
disguise by doing a float, which means giving it little
or no spin. It looks as though there is spin but the
bat contacts the top edge of the ball instead of the
bottom and as it comes down the bat does not slide
underneath the ball.

When Istvan Jonyer does backhand serves he
often leans on his right leg and has his left leg up in
the air. He really uses his body to get sidespin. You
can see something similar in photograph 6. It can
help to get a sharper action. To do this you don't
want to be leaning over the top of the ball or you
will only be able to use your wrist. For this reason
Jonyer sways back a little as he serves.

Many players decide against standing completely
sideways because they might be caught out of position by the return. A server who is not prepared for

17

5

an opponent to do many things with the return may be caught going the wrong way – perhaps expecting the ball to return to a certain place because of the spin on the service, and then finding he is wrong. Sometimes, therefore, it can work to your disadvantage to be the server. There are also limitations to the amount of leg and body action you can get into the service whereas the receiver may be able to use a full body motion for the return.

Control, or spin?

Most leading players aim for control on serve, particularly if they don't have really vicious serves, and also for accurate placement. If they serve with only an average amount of spin, the ball will probably come back, and so will the spin. That will make the third ball much more difficult to play.

Exceptions to this generalization tend to be Chinese players. Most of them have the wrist to produce very spinny serves. They also have to use serves to the greatest advantage because the Chinese often lack certain physical advantages – height and reach. They are usually very effective close to the table where they need to make only short movements, but away from the table they have sometimes

18

6

been at a disadvantage, especially against the three famous Hungarians, Klampar, Jonyer, and Gergely, who are all quite long-legged and long-armed. It has been important for the Chinese to develop their close-to-the-table style with excellent serves and a fast close-to-the-table follow-up. This applies to most players of small stature.

Hold the ball in the flat of the hand (see photo 7).

It is usually best to make contact with the service just over the baseline (see picture C67 in the flicker sequence). How far you should toss it up will vary. Some players send it up three or four inches, others quite high, a few very high indeed – as much as fifteen feet (see Guo Yue-Hua of China on page 25). Everybody tosses the ball differently, depending either on what is most comfortable or what effect they are trying to get. The higher toss tends to facilitate more spin, the lower more control.

Short or long?

Eighty per cent of services should land short. To do this make sure the ball bounces as close to the edge of the table on your side as possible (see photograph C77 in flicker sequence). If it bounces near the net then keeping it short on the other side is impossible.

19

Serve the ball down as close to the edge as possible, get the first bounce short on the other side, and practice so that the second bounce (if it were allowed to) would land on the table. This makes it almost impossible for the receiver to loop, and difficult even to attack. One serve in four, you might serve long as a surprise. Short to the forehand is the hardest position from which to recover for the receiver.

When you risk serving long as a variation it is important to vary things even more by serving with a little topspin. A further variation is the place from which the serve is delivered. Sometimes you should serve from the backhand corner, sometimes from the middle. The great Yugoslav Dragutin Surbek serves a lot with the backhand from the middle, recovering to the backhand side to be ready to play a forehand against any return and from any part of the table. Surbek is tall, with a good reach, and is one of those players with a chance of covering the whole court with his forehand. A smaller player should not take the risk of leaving so much space open and vulnerable.

Where to serve

Varying the direction of the serve is as important as varying the length. Stand in the backhand corner, serve short to the forehand with sidespin or chop, or both; then serve short to the middle. Then try one deep to the forehand if the opponent starts coming in. That may catch him with the ball going awkwardly across his body leaving him only able to push it. Then you could move to the middle and try three different serves from there. This variety, with similar preparation each time, is essential. Another you can try is a little tap-it serve, facing square to the table with the weight evenly distributed. It is simple and has no spin but is often hard for the receiver to do much with. He is left with the task of having to generate all the spin himself.

Another useful variety is the forehand sidespin serve. This is totally different because you turn sideways and crouch down with the left shoulder near to the table (see pictures 8, 9, 10, and 11).

20

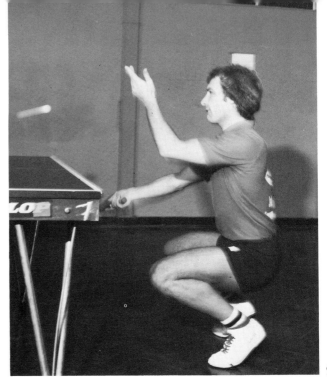

9

10

22

Normally when you serve you have the bat down near the middle of your body. With this one it is up, near your head (see picture 8). You can too bend the wrist back, and make it look as though you are giving the ball a lot of sidespin, but actually chop the ball instead. With this serve you have to be careful not to accidentally toss the ball backwards. This is illegal, although umpires vary in their interpretations of it.

The forehand sidespin serve, in which the bat comes right down on the ball (see picture 10), requires the server to have good strong thighs in order to get back into position again. If a player is not in good shape he or she may only be able to serve from outside the body, instead of from the middle of it, and not be able to crouch so well. This will create more sidespin on the ball but it can still be effective because recovery may be quicker.

The conventional forehand serve, standing up,

1

also requires a sideways stance, or partly sideways. The right leg and the body must be out of the way to allow the bat to go back (see picture 12). The bat comes down inside or underneath the ball, and the body moves round after the bat has gone through. The right leg tends to lift to give more rhythm and attack to the serve. The variations just mentioned can be used with this delivery too. Because you are making contact with the ball outside the body you can really use your wrist, but the serve is likely to be a bit wilder. Backhand serves are almost always tighter and better controlled.

The high toss serve

The forehand serve with a high toss has to be exactly right if you are not to make mistakes. You stand sideways to the table, the bat is flat and close to the body (see picture 13), and the ball can be thrown up anything from four to fourteen feet, which will give much more spin as the ball comes

12

down – provided the ball is contacted right. As the ball goes up, first of all bring the bat above the right shoulder, and come through as though you are going to give it the chop serve again but at the last minute you push the wrist outwards, away from you and up.

13

The secret is to throw the wrist back as far as possible (see picture 14). Then you are able to twist and produce chop as you come through, or you can create topspin. Pushing the wrist outward, away and up creates topspin. It will send the ball cross court from the backhand corner to the other backhand corner. If you want to send the ball down the line you can come round and tilt the bat at the last moment. Hit nearer the bottom of the blade if you are chopping the ball, nearer the top if you are topspinning.

When the ball is coming down from quite a height you do not want a big action or you may miss. The Chinese often just insert the bat into the flight of the ball at the last moment with a tiny movement. Try to make contact close to the body. Throw the ball up above your head and then move away a little so that you strike it where your body was. That helps you to watch the ball and gives you a better body action.

Rule changes

Do not serve from behind the body or prevent your opponent from seeing the ball by hiding it with your body because both became illegal after the rule changes of the 1983–84 season. So did twiddling the bat under the table before serving and stamping to hide the sound of the ball on the bat rubber. To be legal you must also have the ball in the flat of your hand and both ball and bat must be above the table (see picture 7). If you are a combination-bat player you may want to twiddle the bat to create an element of disguise as to which side of the bat and which rubber you want to use. This is still a useful ploy, but you must do it above the table or it will be called a foul serve. (See chapter 17 for further information on combination bats.)

When returning serves it is best to try to develop the habit of taking a calculated risk and of becoming aggressive. Once a player has developed good pushing control, the temptation is to use it because it is safer, but it is better to flick the return. A combination-bat player may find it better to return serves with the anti-spin rubber because that gives more control. He can then flick with his forehand down the line to the backhand. The server will not have much time to move away from the table and get into an attacking position.

Four options

When returning the backhand sidespin serve there are four main options. There is the forehand return down the line, (with anti-loop rubber if you have it). Another is short to the middle (with anti-loop) stopping the opponent getting a good angle. If he tries to push short then move over the table with a backhand hit. A third return, using the reversed rubber, is a chop. That puts the receiver on the defensive. Once the ball is chopped long, the opponent can topspin, provided he has read the rubber and the spin right. He may, though, have to lift the ball which gives the receiver time to go back and defend. The fourth return is playing wide to his forehand (with anti-loop) creating the chance of following up with a smash. If you use anti-loop, the ball is likely to come back high because you have given the opponent no spin.

The most aggressive players will return the serve with the forehand, almost no matter where the serve comes. Their ready position will be in the backhand corner, preparing to play a forehand flick. The flick return is the foundation for a big attack, a way of stopping the opponent getting in with his attack, and a disguise too. It can be used to send the opponent the wrong way.

Chapter 4
Backhand Push

When a beginner picks up a bat, sometimes the only thing he can do is to push the ball on the table. This is a simple, basic shot but one of which to beware. To go on to play at club level or above it is better not to develop the push without having developed other shots as well. Once the habit has been acquired of pushing the blade underneath the ball it is hard to get out of it. It creates a safety-first attitude of merely returning the ball instead of being aggressive.

Modern day coaching stresses the push because it helps development of control. You only have to take the bat back a short distance – no further than the shoulder and sometimes less (see picture A59 in flicker sequence). The backhand push can be played right in front of the body (see picture 15). You don't need to get the body out of the way nor do you need use the wrist, but simply push from the elbow. Simply is the word.

14

The flatter the angle of the bat the more backspin you'll achieve. If you want control, the bat should be at an angle of about 45 degrees, but to get spin the bat will be closer to the horizontal when the ball is struck. If the wrist is broken it will create more spin and a greater variety of effects, but it may cause mistakes. To avoid these, get your head low and keep your eyes close on the ball.

The bat goes down the back and under the ball and makes the ball go round in an anticlockwise direction (called backspin). You can learn to do this in varying amounts to deceive the opponent. When the ball lands it will keep low – the wrist helps to make it do this. The elbow gives more speed.

Transferring weight

Good weight transference also helps. This means the body will move forward with the shot, pushing off the back foot and on to the front foot. Many players try to play the push standing upright but this tends to cause a loss of both speed and control.

How you transfer the weight will depend on your footwork. There are two ways. The orthodox way is to move the right foot across the body; the weight kicks off the left foot as you play the shot, then on to that right foot. This also helps you to get more sideways. However, if you play the backhand push with the left leg slightly forward you can also play the shot with the body much more square to the table (see picture A67 in flicker sequence).

In table tennis, unlike most other sports, it is often not how you prepare for a shot which is most important, but how you come out of it. You must be quickly ready for the next shot because table tennis is such a fast game. Good players may be hitting the ball twice a second for several seconds.

The recovery with the orthodox footwork has to be done right. By putting the right leg slightly across and with the weight on it, you can push off and pivot on the left leg for your next shot. You also get more push by putting the right leg in, and more ability to transfer weight, whereas with the other stance you are a little too square to do all this very well.

29

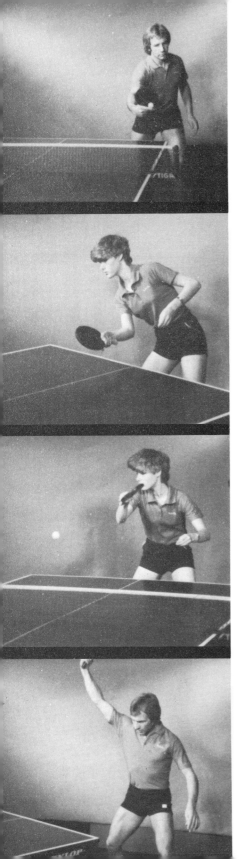

Types of push

There are two main types of push, one short, one long. The short push is often played against a short push or a short serve from the opponent, and will often be just a little touch over the net. Short and low like that it is hard to attack.

This is played from a position further over the table than that of the long push which is usually from nearer the baseline. To reach over the table, the foot may need to go underneath. This time it will have to be the left foot because there will be less room in which to recover. Turning half sideways and back again as you would need to by putting the right foot under would take too long. With the short push you have to move to the ball. With the long push you can often let the ball come to you and then there is more chance to recover. The contact point with a heavy backspin push is more to the bottom of the bat; but with a shot that has little or no spin, nearer to the top.

The backhand push can be used to cover two-thirds of your side of the table. Close-to-the-table shots are often more easily played on the backhand because it is impossible to play a forehand in front of the body. The backhand push can also win a lot of points, particularly if you play with different rubbers (i.e. you are a combination-bat player) because there is less time to see the varieties of spin.

When pushing with an anti-spin rubber the point of contact is different from normal reverse rubbers. If one imagined the ball as a clock face the contact would be made between a quarter to and ten to the hour. This is due to the anti-spin surface not imparting backspin, which would normally pull the ball down and keep it low over the net. Consequently the stroke needs to commence above the ball and make contact with a flat bat and in a 'punching type motion'.

Using these two pushes in different sequences can be very effective, but not everybody will want to use the push a great deal, especially a player using 'normal' rubbers. If you don't wish to defend, it is wise not to use the push much because you may let your opponent on to the attack. Then unless you have a good block, the initiative has gone, and you may have to retreat.

Chapter 5
Forehand Push

Many of the basics for the forehand push are the same for the backhand but in some ways the forehand is the more difficult shot. Firstly, it has to be played outside the body (see Lisa Bellinger, pictures F66 in flicker sequence) and therefore outside the direct line of vision. This is one explanation of why many players serve short to the forehand: the opponent cannot get the eyes directly behind the ball. It is another reason for covering two-thirds of the table with the backhand push.

Secondly, a ball short to the forehand is the hardest point on the table from which to recover. You have to come right into the ball to get control, whereas on the backhand you are able to stretch because your weight is transferred more easily. On the forehand you have the ability to reach more, but at the same time you may be less well balanced and you may leave more of the table open. Also, you can recover from a backhand by reaching for a forehand, but you cannot recover so far when you have to go towards the backhand after playing a forehand.

The forehand push which attempts to gain maximum control will ideally have the bat angle at about 45 degrees to the horizontal (see picture F46 in the flicker sequence). You should use little or no wrist, and bring the left foot across, perhaps turning half sideways. But because of the difficulties in recovering from this shot it is better not to bring the left foot across very far. In the forehand push shown in the flicker sequence Lisa Bellinger has pretty well a square stance. If you are a defensive player you will want to get right down to shots on the forehand, and you can see that Lisa's eyes are very close to the ball in picture F46).

She also appears to move her weight on to her right foot. Many players will tend to put the 'wrong' foot across on the forehand because that is the best way to play the short push. The right foot can then go under the table if necessary (You can see this in picture 16). It would be hard to do this with the left leg.

Only when the ball comes deeper and you don't have to move in really close should you put the left leg forward. That gives you more of a choice as to whether you block or defend on the next shot. When you go forward on the right leg you almost certainly have to follow up with an attack or a block. Then you need to make your opponent reply with another push so that you can get back and loop. It is better not to be caught blocking, unless you are outstanding at it. With the left leg in you are able to push off more quickly to retreat and defend if you need to.

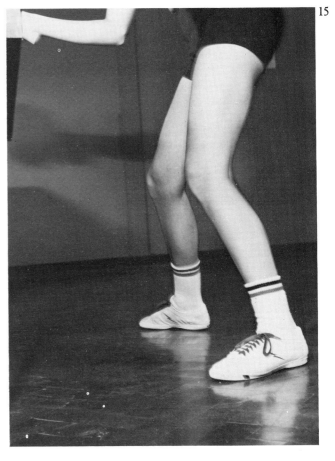

15

Touch shot

If you are involved in a little rally touching the ball over the net on the forehand, you might actually need both legs in. Then you are in a position to flick it, to touch it short, or to really get your head down and push it. Remember, if you are stretching too far, recovery is harder. If your feet are close together you can move away again. On pushing and control shots it is important to be in a compact position.

In a little touch rally it is usual for the right foot to go forward, and then for the left foot to go in when the ball moves over to the backhand side (see picture 17). A few defensive players will not do that because they are quick enough around the table to turn and run the short distance. An attacking player may need only one or two movements to be in a position to play short whereas a defensive player, if he or she is situated a little further away from the table, may have to move three or four steps. The defensive player must also have the physical capacity

16

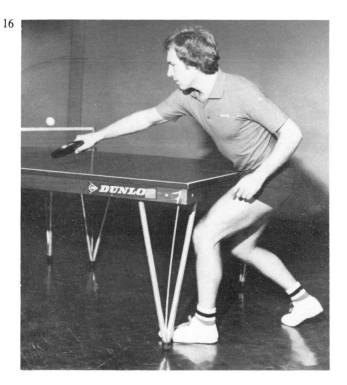

to put the left foot across for the forehand push, and then the right leg across for the other side.

We started with a brief warning about the push and we will finish with another. On the forehand side it is important to develop an attacking mentality. Although a backhand push can cover most of the play when you are really close to the table, a forehand loop or forehand drive can also be used in the same way. A player who is mobile and looking for openings can run round and attack on the forehand a great deal. Therefore it may be best to first learn the backhand push and the forehand hit, and come to the forehand push a little later. But develop a flat hit before you really develop pushing and backspinning into a habit. To that end you should be quickly moving on to learn the block.

Chapter 6
Backhand Block

The block illustrates what modern table tennis is about – not relinquishing the initiative and getting back on to attack as soon as possible. Despite this the game has developed so much that the block should only be used sparingly. At one time the game was all defence, push, push, and then it was all block, block, all counter-hit. After that there developed counter-hit on the backhand and smash on the forehand, then topspin on the forehand and topspin on the backhand. The block is still important, but only briefly, to regain the initiative. At a beginner's level, however, it is a useful way of developing the basis of a flat hit and a drive.

Although blocking requires good reflexes it is essential for most players to try to develop the shot, and it can and should be brought in at an early stage of a player's development. It can be learnt with the bat tilted over the ball, not upright and perpendicular to the table. In that way it can be developed into a slightly rolled over shot, with a little topspin. That is the way Klampar does it, in an offensive way. If a young player develops this from the beginning it will be far better. You start to turn your bat over, using your body to move with the shot. The counter-hit has similarities to this kind of block.

However, a beginner should wait for the ball to come to him, and not go looking for it. Try to guide it and to acquire the basic control and turn-over of the wrist which is important. Also learn to use the full arm and open up the face of the bat. Stellan Bengtsson and Ulf Thorsell, the two Swedes, have been perfect examples. They obtained a lot of power from the forearm and also a lot of control by knocking the spin off.

The best way is to open up, let the ball come into the face of the bat, and then turn it slightly over. But don't turn the wrist, turn the forearm. A lot of

players just flap the wrist, which is no good. To do it properly the timing must be perfect but after a while that will come. It is a quick quarter turn of the bat and the legs and body move with the arm.

To obtain the feel of this action the beginner should turn the forearm (wrist and arm) and lay it flat on the table. Once he has the feeling of this and has built it into the shot he has an aggressive block. The controlled block is when you already have your bat in the turned-over position and it is held there. The difference between the block and the backhand counter-hit is that the block is a shorter shot – you let the ball come to you. And the counter-hit is played higher, the block lower. You can take the block early, sometimes as the ball is coming up, sometimes on the half-volley.

When to use it

There are two obvious situations where the block may most profitably be used. One is when your opponent is looping into your backhand from his forehand side, and you can't get round to forehand topspin back against him. Then you come in and block it down the line. There may be a gap there on his forehand and even though he reaches it he may have to throw the ball up, and then you can get in and smash. The other situation is when your opponent gets in the first topspin while you are close to the table, and the block is returned hard back across into his body. Then if this makes him play a half topspin or even a backhand, you can come in with your own topspin.

In top table tennis a player should not really be blocking two shots in a rally. One is enough. An out and out blocker does not often win top matches because so many opponents have the power to hit through that style. Even Desmond Douglas, one of the best and most famous blockers in the game, developed a good forehand looped topspin with which to attack first. Topspin has been developed so much in the modern game that you cannot do without it.

However early on in the rally, off the third,

36

fourth, and fifth balls, a player is usually still so close to the table that he has no choice but to block. If the opponent topspins he can either block or go for a smash, though the latter is taking a chance against a topspin ball. In this situation there will probably not be the room to topspin against topspin, which is the reply often used these days.

The backhand block should be developed, but the forehand block should be limited because on that side a player ought to be learning to hit or counter-hit, or to topspin. If you are caught blocking on the forehand there is usually something wrong, and it is better to cut the shot out from an early stage in your career. Then your mind will be more geared to getting your right leg back, and giving yourself room on the forehand for a smash or a topspin.

If you develop a style in which the weight is anchored on your right leg and you are covering much of the table with your backhand, you will become restricted. You don't have time to transfer the weight for the forehand. Close to the table the weight should be evenly distributed between the two feet, or on the left leg. Then you can pivot on the left leg and get round quickly for a forehand attack.

Sensitivity

As you improve you learn to become more and more sensitive with the block. You learn to block it back short to stop the opponent looping again and to cushion the ball with the bat. And you can learn to feel the ball on to the bat and make the impact softer, slightly drawing the bat back on impact. It is probably easier to get this type of feeling with the penholder grip. With the penholder you are using no arm action and you have the hand behind the bat to help give more feeling. Most of the Chinese penholder players have been good blockers, especially Li Chen-Shih and Jiang Jia-liang.

To play this shot well you have to be very sensitive to the kind of spin on the ball and be able to alter the angle of your bat accordingly. For instance, if you are blocking a topspin the bat is more closed (see picture 18 and picture 19) and if you are blocking against a flat hit the bat is more

37

17

18

38

perpendicular. Sometimes it will be almost horizontal, i.e. when you are having to contain a very heavily topspun ball. If it is a high topspin then you also have to get above it and force it down. If it is a topspin that the opponent has played at the top of the bounce – a fast drive topspin rather than a high topspinning loop – you can leave the bat face more open and you will still have the control you need. You will then be able to use the opponent's speed to angle the ball away.

What normally happens is that the first player to get in with a topspin is seventy-five per cent of the way towards winning the point. If the blocker manages to return it well, where he wants to, then the chances of winning the point are fifty-fifty. It may be even higher in favour of the blocker if, as he plays the shot, he can also get away from the table quickly. If he does that he is ready for anything.

Chapter 7
Backhand and Forehand Hits and Drives

The backhand and forehand hits and drives are important for all kinds of players. For beginners they are good, useful, basic, and relatively simple, and can be the basis of the development of other important shots. With a little more roll and body action a hit can become a drive.

These shots can be important for all kinds of advanced players too – attackers and defenders. The Chinese in the early eighties developed a flat attack after service that often won the point immediately, and if necessary was followed up by a devastating smash. A flat attack can be used to stop the server as well. A defender needs a good hit to put the ball away after the push or chop has caused the opponent to misread the spin and return the ball too high. In these situations the backhand hit can be used to cover about three-quarters of the table.

A good hit or drive is also useful for a modern combination-bat player. By using anti-spin on the backhand drive the effect is, instead of creating a little topspin as often happens, of hitting it flat. Even with the reversed pimples you can do the same flat hit if the shot is executed properly. Instead of coming over the ball with your wrist, the shot goes more or less straight through it.

How to do the backhand hit

The backhand hit is played standing fairly square to the table (picture 20). If it is used against the service you can go in with either foot first. But if it is used in a rally the weight should be on the left foot to help gain the full force of the body. Don't use too much wrist because it is more of a flat hit you need. You punch the ball, but you don't turn the bat over and you need to use the body to force the ball forwards.

40

19

20

21

You can only take the bat back as far as your chest on the backhand, so you do not get much power from the backswing. Neither should power come from playing outside the body and trying to take the bat back further. If you play backhand shots out there you have to use the wrist to obtain control. Then it is more of a loop. Instead, try to come down on the ball, rather than strike the back. You have to be very aware that you need to hit down and flat or you will put topspin on it. So you really have to get in a position above the ball to play the backhand hit properly.

It is therefore best to make contact quite close to the table, probably no more than a foot away (see picture 20A) otherwise you will start to use wrist. The wrist is straight. Most of the shot should come from the forearm. The arm does not move a great deal from the shoulder, but more from the elbow. A lot of players bring the bat back horizontally, but better to bring it back vertical so that it lies on the chest flat, then it goes through flat. You follow through all the way, which is perhaps the most important part of the shot (picture 21) because it enables the bat to stay on the ball longer.

Where to hit it

As you can see from the flicker sequence the ball can be directed across court and down the line with a similar action on the backhand hit, creating disguise and thus often producing a winner. To hit the ball cross-court is easier because the weight is going that way. When you hit down the line you have to use more of the arm and so it is difficult to hit the ball as hard or as flat. But if it is done with deception, it will not matter. You would probably use the one down the line when you are dominating a right-handed opponent in the backhand corner, and he is looking to move round to use the forehand. Try to pin him down on the backhand, and if you see he wants to move round then play it down the line. What happens is that instead of following right through the shot, fade across the ball (see pictures E30, E28 and E26 in the flicker sequence). You also play the ball a little shorter. That should make

42

it safer for you should he be able to recover to reach it with his forehand because he will be less likely to be able to do a full-blooded loop.

This disguised backhand hit can also be used if the opponent does get round and loop the ball with his forehand into your backhand. You may not then have time to play the complete shot, but instead produce a block-hit (with anti-spin rubber if you use it). You move away again when you make contact so that you have room to attack the next ball. If the opponent hits the ball flat or with a rolled topspin instead of a loop you will be able to punch the backhand hit because there will not be a lot of spin coming at you.

Which rubbers to use

The punched backhand hit down the line is played with reversed pimples (the normal) side of the bat. It is taken very early, just off the bounce instead of letting the ball come to the top of the bounce. If you are using the anti-spin rubber you have to let the ball come as high as you can, once again with the effect of a downwards hit. Picking the ball up earlier enables you to make use of the faster material, and perhaps to put some topspin on the ball. Then it becomes a kind of topspin block-hit. Speed will partly come from the pace on the opponent's shot.

With the dead anti-spin rubber and a good backhand hit you have a chance of being able to do something with almost any service. You can probably hit or flick even if the serve is heavily chopped or sidespun. You can mentally destroy a lot of opponents whose game is based round a good service, an easy return, and a good follow-up. With this technique and material you can destroy a third ball attack.

These days more and more players are flicking or hitting against the service, even without the anti-spin rubber. Not so many returns are pushed these days because then you are liable to have a ball topspun quickly at you. The modern technique is to hit or flick because if the return of serve is not forcing you can lose a lot of quick points.

Backhand or forehand?

A defender will often use a backhand hit when he has been away from the table and is running back in. If you are running in for a drop shot or a half-hit ball then the backhand hit is very useful because you can play it immediately in front of you as you are moving. You can also cover most of the table with this shot. It takes a lot longer to get in position to hit the forehand because you have to get to the table and then get your body round the side of the table. It is also harder to recover after playing a forehand hit. If the ball is blocked back the body is probably still over the table, and to the side. Thus you need more time both after and before the forehand to be able to recover position.

22

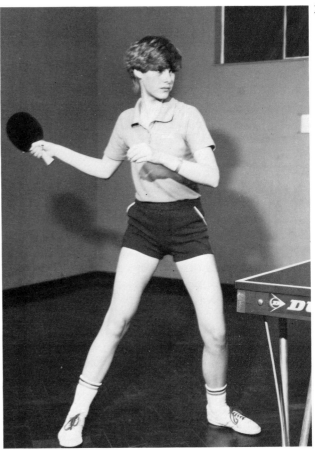

Despite this the forehand hit is very often the winning shot. You can put more effort into it because you can take the bat further back and get more power from the shoulders. And you can turn sideways and swivel right round and transfer your weight more (see picture 22). It can become a really dominating shot with all that body movement, back-swing, and follow-through. Yet it is still the more chancy shot – the greater the effort the less time you have for recovery if the ball is blocked back. By contrast the backhand hit is a quicker, smaller, safer movement.

Nevertheless the backhand hit can be an important shot. Many players, especially with close-to-the-table styles, use it to dominate the rally and put the ball away with the forehand. These days, that put-away would often be done by looping the ball off the bounce – a fast topspin drive. But if the ball was put up high and loose then a forehand hit would be used. Particularly will it be used if you get in a good spin which the opponent misreads. If, for instance, you deliver a good serve and he makes a topspin return, it may be very difficult for him to keep the ball down if the ball pops up and the forehand hit or forehand smash comes in.

There is one other point that applies to both the backhand and forehand hit. Many players are coached cross-court practice sequences, which can become a bad habit. The diagonal cross court is easier – there is a bigger distance to hit into – but you are more likely to find a hole in the opponent's defence if you hit down the line. When under pressure most people tend to revert to habits, so don't practise or play crosscourts endlessly. Better to feint to hit across court, throw your shoulders that way, but move the bat the other way. That's how you can catch a lot of players out.

Chapter 8
Forehand Loop

The biggest single factor in table tennis is to be able to get an attacking stroke in, and to get it in first. Just about the most aggressive stroke of all is the forehand loop, or the forehand topspin, and you can use the shot against many returns. The smash is harder and faster, and so sometimes is the block, but these strokes can only be used off certain balls. That's why the loop is the most important.

It has also become the stroke that changed table tennis. Whoever gets in first using today's attacking rubbers is likely to dominate the rally, and gradually defenders have become both less effective and less common. Frequently a loop attack will start on the third shot of the rally, as a follow-up to the service.

It is a big action shot. To prepare for it, first turn sideways, drop the bat down within a few inches of the floor, and as you bring it up quickly you brush the back of the ball, and transfer your weight forwards. There is a sensation of gripping as the rubber strikes the ball. Topspin comes from a combination of wrist, arm and body.

The secret of speed

One of the big secrets of the loop, which a lot of players forget, is to get used to bending (see picture 23). A lot of players just leave their bat down low and then they risk getting stuck. If you get down as far as you can, so that you are almost sitting, then you can generate much more speed. Speed comes with the bat as you come up. Power comes from the legs as they straighten. Follow-through goes above the head (picture 24).

You also get speed from the wrist, which you drop and then bring quickly up and through. But try not to get into the situation of just using the

46

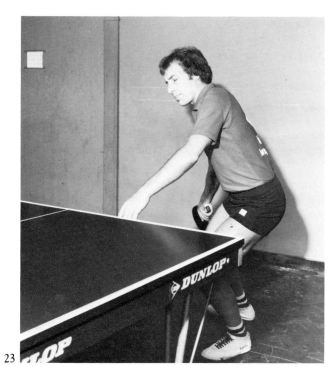

23

24

wrist to get the ball over the net (flicking it). It will probably be best to have the face of the bat open and then come over the top of the ball with the wrist, but make sure you do all the other things right. If it is a difficult ball, pushed or chopped with backspin and keeping low, then you will have to lift the ball up more than a ball blocked flat, or hit with topspin. Then you may need to let the ball drop a little before making contact.

When the ball comes long, so that the second bounce would drop over the end of the table, that is when you have a chance of looping it. You must get in position quickly. You may not achieve a perfect position but if you are committed, which you should be, then you must play the shot. In such a situation you need to adjust.

Get your body moving first because it can produce great power (see pictures B31, B33, B35, B37 and B39 in the flicker sequence). Then the arm, wrist, shoulders, and elbow all come through. Try to have the eyes and the body behind the ball, so you can judge better its bounce and speed. If the ball comes quickly to you and it is going to bounce high, you will need to get above the ball and hit down (see picture AA).

Coordinating

Even against a push a lot of players are able to put everything into the loop. The lower you bend the more lift you can give the shot, and you can also rotate the shoulders (see pictures B51, B53, B55, B57, B59 in the flicker sequence). Get your feet into position first and then your shoulders will automatically go round. Feet ready, body, shoulders, then arm, then wrist. That's how speed, power and spin come. You can only really use your wrist properly if the rest of your body is in coordination.

There are three different types of loop – high and kicking, low and fast, and sidespin loops. Which you use will depend upon which kind of ball you are receiving – looping a push, looping a loop, etc. If you are looping a heavily chopped ball and you have to lift it more, you will use the bottom half of the blade and the trajectory of the bat will be more vertical. The result will be a high and kicking loop.

Looping the loop has a discus-type action and produces a lower, faster shot. This is a drive-loop, and the middle-to-top section of the blade makes contact and the bat goes more horizontal. Looping from the block requires contact at the *back* of the ball because it will be a fast ball coming at you.

The forehand loop from a push or flick, on the third stroke in the rally, is what the modern game is based around. Most top players use it. On the third ball the loop is a closer, more compact shot. If the opponent blocks it, step away to give yourself more room for the fifth shot. Then the ball is coming to you instead of you going to meet it.

This backward movement of course affects where you put your weight, which will now be more on the back foot, which is different from looping against a heavily chopped ball, when your weight will probably be coming forwards. This shot also needs the body moving in to knock the spin off the ball and get more power.

Commitment

If your bat is in an open position, you can play the shot just with your arm, but once the bat is turned over you have to use your body. You have to generate forward movement. Turning the bat into the discus position forces you to use your body. The technique commits you. This is the essential point – the Japanese commit themselves one hundred per cent when they play, which is why they are so aggressive and a nation to be feared. Almost no matter which Japanese player you meet you know he will commit himself and straightaway put you under pressure.

Some players are developing the topspin loop immediately off the bounce (instead of at the top of the bounce) but this is dangerous to try because the timing has to be perfect. Most players allow the ball to rise to its full height and possibly drop again before topspinning. This makes the shot easier but allows the opponent more time to recover. If the ball is dropping there is however more chance of missing it completely, so be careful to make contact.

In the early 1970s the block was used to counter topspin, but since then the block has not been as

effective and players are now topspinning against topspin. One day the game may be all forehand topspin off the bounce. With pimpled rubber (where the ball stays on the rubber a lot longer), the smash against the topspin can be developed. The Chinese always look for chances to use the smash. Their technique and recovery always makes them ready to smash the next ball, which makes them very dangerous. We in England need develop the two styles together, the Chinese and the Hungarian all-looping style, whereas we have tended to develop only the Hungarian.

The Hungarians have nevertheless been brilliant at looping. The former world champion Istvan Jonyer and the former European champion Gabor Gergely played with a very relaxed arm, whereas the English tend to be a bit stiff and tense. The Hungarians really open up. They are square to the table after they have looped. They have opened up the body.

Don't stop on it

Quick recovery when looping close to the table is essential because your opponent may try to block. There can be a tendency to stop on the loop because of the fear that the ball will come back quickly. That is fatal. Getting the first loop in gives an advantage and you must try to take it. The follow-through should go right through high above the head, with a straight arm as far as it can go. Then you are committed (see picture B89 in the flicker sequence). Jonyer and Klampar almost always do this. If you stop and try to recover that's when you don't put spin on the ball.

Many players do start the rally with a more compact, shorter arm movement and then build up. Close to the table there may not be room for a full-blooded shot. But then they move further away the longer the rally goes on. Some players like to step back before winding up for the loop. Gergely, for instance, when blocking, will already be moving away. Jonyer loops out in front of himself to enable him to get away from the table and make more room. Even if you do get in a good first loop you can be caught out of position by a quick return, especially if you loop down the lines. Many players, including Jonyer, loop down the middle to stop the opponent getting an angle.

Great as the Hungarians have been the Chinese style is more likely to be the one of the future. Those players who have concentrated only on top-spin are realizing that they may have missed the boat, because coaches are now bringing on young players who are developing both the loop and the smash. Erik Lindh, the Swede, has a fantastic topspin and a fantastic smash, and as time goes by all but the very best loopers can forget top table tennis unless they have both.

Chapter 9
Backhand Loop

Players tend to use a forehand loop against a fore-hand loop because it is usually more difficult to topspin the backhand. On the forehand you can pick the ball up immediately after the bounce, or perhaps a few inches later, but on the backhand it is difficult to adjust once you are committed. Apart from that, players these days are often fit enough to run round to play the forehand from the backhand side and still cover the rest of the table.

The backhand loop does though have some advantages. Pengrip players can be placed under pressure by European shake-hand grip players because the cross-court backhand loop goes straight into the penholder's awkward spot. The Swedes, the Poles and the Czechs, as well as the famous Hungarians have all developed it. Against such players it becomes very, very rare that you get an easy ball because every return will have topspin on it, on both backhand and forehand. And this is the way table tennis is likely to continue. In the past ten years the perfect example has been Gergely, a player with a good block, who after using it steps away from the table and employs his power game, looping both forehand and backhand.

Coaches say that if the ball is pushed, the back-hand loop should be played in the middle of the body, square on, with the left leg slightly forward. That is because it is the easiest position if you have to adjust. When the ball is played long the first thing is to get into a position from which you can adapt. Once you know the ball is on your backhand you must get down into a sitting position. Above all do not look at the ball and make a premature decision about where to move because the game is played too quickly for that.

52

Control and compromise

Once into position with the feet, the body is well placed to adjust depending on where the ball is. You can play the backhand loop in the area in front of your body, or even slightly outside the body. But the loop outside the body should only be used against a blocked return, or in a loop-the-loop rally.

If you are down into a sitting position (see picture H56 in the sequence) it is easier to control the backhand loop, but because you have to be behind the shot you may have less manoeuvrability. After your legs are in position you can only sway from side to side. Despite that players often control it just as well by swaying into the shot. But you can't compensate with your arm and your wrist as you can on the forehand.

If the ball is pushed to you then the backhand loop is similar to the forehand. You have to get underneath the ball. The loop with the bat horizontal and completely closed – turned right over – is no good. Open the bat and let the ball come on to it and then turn it over.

How the bat goes down in preparation for the shot depends on the leg movement – not the arm, as some might think – and elasticity in your legs helps to get a lot more spin, variation and power. The Hilton loop tends to have control from the wrist. This also gives spin, but there is not much arm or body action, and with a wristy loop the bat doesn't go very low, perhaps only to about knee height (see picture H66). This is a loop close to the table played against a pushed or flicked ball.

Close to the table

Close to the table most players use the wrist because of the control it gives and because that assists the need to be ready to play the ball quicker. The feet have to be into position immediately, followed by a quick action. Once the player moves away from the table and starts to loop against a blocked ball, or to loop the loop, then it is a different technique.

If you're good enough, you can play the backhand loop out round the side – outside the body – as a lot

53

of players now do. You can see it in picture 25. The Poles have developed it so that they can twist the body and really open up. They don't use too much wrist, and have a straight arm. Then the shot is easier that way round.   They get a lot of power that way. If you try to use your wrist you are only flicking, and what's more, only flicking when you are a distance away from the table. In this situation you need more power: you dare not flick the ball up or you allow your opponent time to come in and smash. Instead you must give the ball power to keep it low. Doing that with your wrist is too difficult. It is the body and arm that are needed (see picture 26).

The backhand discus with the bat turned over the ball is a difficult shot because it is not easy to get body into the shot while it is very easy to miss the ball altogether. Despite this Andrzej Grubba of Poland has a more powerful loop on this side than on the forehand and one of the main reasons is because he commits himself one hundred per cent. The backhand discus loop can be done well, and when it is, it sometimes makes the difference between a top player and the others.

Chapter 10
Forehand Sidespin Loop

The forehand sidespin loop is also a useful shot in a different way. Instead of being the shot you get in first it is valuable as a counter. If done well it makes the ball deviate a lot, which makes it hard to answer. It tends to produce a cross-court reply to the forehand, so obviously if you are not strong on that wing it is not to be recommended. But it is a particularly effective shot against a blocker, who will find the sidespin makes it hard for him to time the ball properly.

Some players generate sidespin by using their arm to take the bat round the outside of the ball. It is, though, frequently better to produce a more committed stroke, taking the bat round the body, a little like discus, and bringing the body and the right leg round with it. You can see this in pictures 27, 28, and 29. It helps to cock the wrist as well. You can afford to commit yourself a good deal more with this type of loop because you have a good idea where the ball is coming back – cross court. The sidespin loop is difficult both to play and return down the line.

If the ball is coming hard at you it is better to try to loop at the top of the bounce rather than lower because that tends to produce a scoop. Against a block, play the sidespin loop somewhere between the chest and the waist. Against a topspin it can be played lower, even perhaps at knee height. In this situation it can be especially effective because you are just guiding the ball round and therefore you have the ball on the surface of the bat longer, making control easier.

It is, though, a speciality shot. It can get you out of trouble, and it troubles the blocker as we said, because he cannot return the ball where he wants to on the table. But beware: if you rely more on sidespin than topspin against 'loop-the-loop' players you will be in trouble.

56

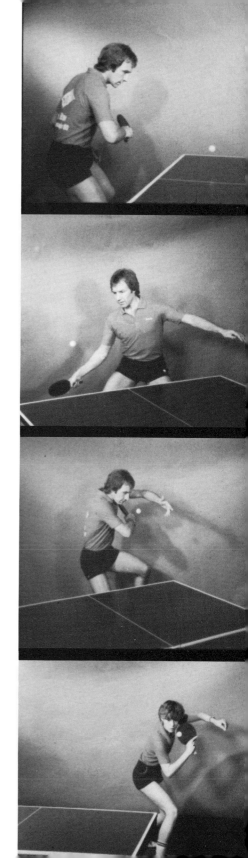

Chapter 11
Forehand Kill or Smash

It is essential that the smash is learnt properly because its importance has greatly increased. In the early seventies topspin was developed and the loop became the shot all young players coming into the game had to play. Coaches helped them develop it and the smash tended to be neglected. Because the three brilliant Hungarians, Jonyer, Gergely, and Klampar went on to win both the world and European championships with their topspin loops everybody was loosening their wrists, dropping their arms and topspinning.

But things have changed. Players now are a lot fitter. The physical side is much more important and the game has become very much a matter of getting into position quickly. Some of those players who concentrated on topspin have realized they have missed the boat, because the coaches are now bringing on players who are developing not only topspin but also the smash.

Look at Erik Lindh, of Sweden – fantastic topspin, fantastic smash. Many of the top junior players today have both. All but the top loopers can forget being successful unless they have both. Once a good blocker knows you can only topspin he feels much more confident about getting the ball back.

The value of the smash or the forehand kill is that it gives the opponent less time to read what is going to happen. That is because the ball is struck flat, and therefore comes at him quicker. Normally the smash is a follow-up after topspin, although Chinese players such as Cai Zhen-hua and Xie Saike often use a flat attack immediately after service. It is best to develop flat and topspin shots. If, however, one shot has to be developed before the other it should be the smash first, and the topspin afterwards. It is easier that way round

Balance and pivot

To learn the smash, keep the bat above the table instead of letting it drop. Bring the left leg across, so that the shoulders come round to a sideways position (see picture G70 in the sequence). This gives sufficient balance so that the contact point can vary, depending on the speed and the height of the ball. Bringing the shoulders round also gives you the power to really open out, and the choice as to whether you want to hit the ball softly with control, or as hard as you can.

If you leave the leg where it is, then you are committed as to where and how you strike the ball. Bringing it across provides the ability to pivot – as you see Lisa Bellinger doing in the flicker sequence (pictures G40, G42, G44). You can then play the ball early, you can play it late, and you can wait. Without this you have a limited choice, and limited speed as well – only that which the arm alone can generate. You lose much of the ability to transfer weight from the back foot to the front, and that is more important in this shot than in any other. If you don't get round properly the shot is more like a controlled block than a kill.

It is probably best to drop the wrist so that your arm is perfectly straight. If you look down the forearm, everything should be in line from the shoulder to the wrist. If the wrist is cocked – brought up – then that is normally the looping position. But with the kill there is a straight line – shoulder, elbow, wrist, with the wrist stiff – although you can bend the elbow as Lisa does in the sequence. Dropping the wrist tends to stop you using too much wrist. Instead you use your body. By contrast, with a topspin shot you use more of a relaxed wrist enabling the ball to be played almost anywhere.

Open or closed?

A very important point concerns the angle of the bat face. When you are topspinning you can manage with it either facing downwards or being vertical. But when you are smashing, once the leg and the shoulders are round, you should open the face of the

59

bat. Only then can the ball be struck flat and in the middle.

Once you let the bat close you start to commit yourself, your body weight comes in, you are on the way. However, if you keep it open you have more choice. You can then take the ball just off the bounce, or later if you please. Players who have got into the habit of only looping the ball always tend to have a closed bat, no matter how suitable for smashing it is. As soon as the ball comes towards them the bat is down, they are coming over the top and they never think of opening the bat at all. If you do open the bat it makes you get up above the ball, because you have to lift your shoulder and your elbow.

You can smash both a low and a high ball, although the techniques are sometimes different. With a high ball it is essential to make sure you get above the ball, and to get up higher you may even need to jump. Then the weight comes down heavily on the left leg. You should also jump off this same leg. If you don't your weight will be on the other leg and you will then be restricted to only one contact point, whereas with the left leg round you can decide between various possibilities.

Height and room

How high you take the ball depends on the situation you are in. Away from the table the ball may come up to you higher. Close to the table you may need to give yourself room. Decide quickly where you are going to try to make contact because it is often too late to go backwards.

If you have the two techniques of topspin and kill, try to give yourself room to do either. If you are always close to the table and always dropping the wrist, you can only topspin. If you give yourself room by using topspin and then moving away, you can if necessary step back in and kill, and you can still topspin. But if you topspin close to the table the ball is usually too near to your body to smash.

At advanced level it is particularly important to be able to get away from the table after you have made your shot. This is something to be remembered when doing physical training. It helps to practise movements where you push off backwards, because nearly half the time in modern table tennis that is what you are doing.

It is important that your kill be full-blooded. Get sideways and follow-through right across the body to the left side of your head. If you try to disguise the kill too much, you may tend to stop on the ball. And if you are square on, you will not be able to follow-through properly. You should not of course commit yourself to a follow-through that makes you vulnerable to a good block. Normally, though, an opponent faced with a really full-blooded kill will go away from the table to create a better chance of returning the ball. This should give time for the smasher to recover no matter how much follow-through is used. Therefore, if in doubt go for the kill, and risk it. See picture 29A, which shows Desmond Douglas doing a jump smash.

9a

Chapter 12
The Chop

Defending with chop and float is used less in international play these days – unfortunately for table tennis as a spectacle. If they defend, players are more likely to throw the ball back with topspin. Despite this, chop and float is still a useful part of the game and a good all-round player will find it valuable. By varying your defence – especially if you use a combination bat (with different rubbers on each side) – you can sometimes be successful against the big loopers.

The first point about chopping is that by bringing your bat back flat you can control the ball, no matter how much topspin is on it. With the bat flat in your hand you are forced to use the wrist to get any forward motion. That knocks the spin off the ball. If you bring the bat back to a vertical position you have almost no control as a defensive player.

Ideally you move your body across and into the shot with the shoulder sideways to the table. The front leg (for a right-hander on the forehand chop this is the left leg), should come across. This enables you to bend your right knee. As you prepare you will be almost crouching. Take the wrist back as far as it will go, and the bat back from the elbow and a little from the shoulder. Strike the ball just above the front knee and level with it. Make contact near the bottom of the blade down the back and underneath the ball. That will give the ball heavy backspin.

Right leg across

Players who are slow or who simply use the wrong technique sometimes put the right leg across. You can manage a forehand chop like this, but it doesn't really allow you to bend because your weight is all on that right foot. As a result you can't use your body to move into the shot. When the left leg is moved across the weight is better distributed between the feet and you can bend more easily without putting strain on knees and thighs. One advantage of the wrong technique is that you can recover more quickly to a ready position (see picture 30).

Control comes mostly from the wrist. The bat goes up level with the shoulder and slightly behind the head. Though the bat goes back from the elbow you don't use too much elbow: mostly the bat comes round with the body. The follow-through has to be exaggerated as far as it will go.

30

If this produces a chop with a lot of backspin it can be used aggressively to prevent the looper from attacking properly. It forces him to use his loop simply to lift up a backspinning ball. The chop can also be used to knock spin off the ball when the looper is attacking hard. Then the follow-through is especially important. If you knock off the spin and don't follow through the ball will just die. It won't even reach the table.

Getting down to it

It will be harder to do all these things when you just put that right foot across instead of getting round with the left. Then you stand square to the table, from which position it will be more difficult to get underneath the ball with the wrist. If you are in position to get the angle of the bat as far back as you can – by getting your legs down to the ball – you can really knock the spin off. If you don't get down, you will have to close the angle of the bat a little (so it is more vertical). Then if there is topspin on the ball it will be difficult to control.

The first reaction under pressure is very often to reach across, which is a habit you should break as soon as possible. First move the feet and then get down and reach, because then you can adjust. You can't adjust to the height and speed of the ball if you have already committed yourself and started the shot. If you reach first it's too late because you are halfway into the shot. You can then only play it away from you with your arm extended, losing control.

On the forehand chop the timing must be perfect, in contrast to the backhand chop which is safer because you are behind the ball (see picture 31). The forehand is played outside the body – riskier but it enables you to put more chop into it. If you are using one of the 'normal' reversed rubbers the forehand chop has to be just right. Good players (assisted sometimes by anti-spin rubber on the backhand) can vary the timing and the point of contact because they have more control. Anti-spin rubber assists this because, as the name says, it kills the spin. We talk more about materials, and combination bats – very important for a chopper – at a later stage.

Square or sideways?

The backhand chop can be played square on, as can many of the other backhand shots. When playing with anti-spin and not putting spin on the ball yourself, it is wiser not to retreat too far from the table. However, as you see from Lisa Bellinger's position in the sequence, you get more backspin if you are sideways (picture D77). Once again, the knees should be forward, and the weight off the back foot. Even when playing the shot very defensively the weight must still be transferred from the back foot to the front. This is an important point with most shots.

On the backhand chop the bat can come up pretty well to the shoulder (see picture 32). Again the angle of the bat should be flat, or as far back as it will go, to help you kill the spin. And again, take it back from the wrist as far as possible, but only a little from the elbow and the shoulder (see picture D33 in the sequence). Make contact just in front of the front foot. Balance is all-important. The follow-through with the backhand naturally brings the arm across the body whereas the follow-through on the

65

forehand it cannot do so. You may recover better from the backhand chop because your arm is on the side of the body that towards which the recovery is made.

If you play the backhand chop square-on, almost straight in front of your body, the back swing is shorter. It is a smaller, more compact shot, with less wrist. Nor do you follow-through as far. Recovery, though, is less of a problem. You can keep the bat there, just in front of you, and you can often take smaller steps to the ball. Once defensive players see the ball is on the forehand they tend to open out and stride towards it and then they are almost falling into the shot. On the backhand you can sometimes get away with moving the bat first and then moving the feet. On the forehand once you reach out with the bat it affects adversely the other movements. You can no longer get down to the ball.

Backspin is created by striking the ball with the bottom part of the bat. To create a lot of backspin, strike the bottom of the ball. Timing needs to be perfect to contact the absolute bottom; usually it is a little above the bottom. There is, however, another way of making contact – with the middle or top of the bat. This is the float.

The float

A float looks like a chop but in fact gives no spin. Because the opponent plays for a ball with spin, a float causes him to return it too high, creating the chance to finish the rally with a kill. The angle of the bat on the float is as important as the contact point. You don't close it, but keep the bat at about forty-five degrees to the floor. Instead of following through the bat tends to go towards the floor – more in a downwards direction instead of down and up. But it is often hard for the opponent at the other end to see the difference between this and the follow through for the chop – a difference that is obvious if you are watching from the side. Sometimes, too, the follow-through goes below the height of the table, where it cannot be seen. The float can therefore be mixed very profitably with chop. If one ball is played with a lot of spin and the next with no spin, a defender has suddenly become aggressive because the opponent has to cope with many different balls. The float has a further advantage of being the easiest shot to make. Producing a ball with no spin does not make such demands upon getting into position. Very often you only have to get your bat to the ball and that will do.

It is important that a defensive player knows which balls he can spin and how much. If the ball is thrown high with topspin the defensive player will have time to get into position, and he is given a choice. However, if the ball has a lot of spin he may not be able to read it, and the normal practice is not to chop too heavily. When a ball is dropping short it will be difficult for a defender to spin it because he has to come underneath it low to the floor. On the other hand if it already has heavy spin he will return it too high if he gives it no spin at all.

67

Playing against defence

If an attacker produces topspin when meeting a defensive player for the first time it will probably be returned with no spin at all. If he produces a high topspin ball it will probably be returned with a degree of backspin. If he gives a ball with only a little spin and not a lot of speed then the returning spin will certainly be more severe. This happens if the attacker is not in position and just loops the ball up. That is a situation in which some say the chopper is not really defending but attacking, because he is controlling the rally and forcing the opponent to use the loop simply to get the ball back on the table.

Conversely, if a defensive player receives fierce topspin when out of position then he will have difficulty in getting the ball back on the table with control. A defensive player may have to face fast low topspin, high heavy topspin, or high slight topspin, and the test of how good he is is whether he can use the appropriate technique for any given situation.

The normal defensive tactic is that the further the ball travels before it is returned, the less spin there is likely to be on it. Then the defender can control the spin or dictate how he wants to return the ball. If he tries to return it when it has maximum spin, then he may not be able to decide what kind of spin he wants to impart. If he waits, some of the spin will leave the ball.

When playing against choppers, watch the wrist. If you see a quick action then you know the ball is chopped. If you see a slow action and a downwards follow-through, it is floated. With combination bat players the action can be the same for both chop and float. In these situations you can try to listen for the sound. There is a difference between the noise of the ball on anti-spin rubber and either reversed rubber or long pimpled rubber. You can also look out for the different colour on each side, different colours being obligatory since the rule changes in 1984. You can inspect his bat before the match, to see the rubber. Watch the flight of the ball. A chopped ball is more likely to stay low over the net whereas sometimes a floated ball may travel in more

68

of an arc. Then you can also look for the action of the wrist: the chopped stroke goes underneath the ball, the chop with pimples or anti-spin rubber is nearer to the vertical, probably at about forty-five degrees. It is played quickly but if you watch closely you can sometimes see it.

Rubbers and spins

If defensive players use the reversed rubber, then normally the ball will be chopped. If they use the anti-spin or pimples the ball may be floated. But players have also developed a new technique and tactic whereby they use the normal (reversed rubber) side but don't chop. Instead of playing the ball on the bottom of the bat and following through, they play it on the top of the bat and give it no spin. This can catch offensive players out. However, some players have good enough eyesight to look at the label on the ball as it comes towards them. If it isn't clear they know the ball has spin on it!

A defensive player with a combination bat is usually less dangerous away from the table. But if the opponent pushes and the combination bat defender comes back into the table and pushes, he becomes dangerous. It is then harder to pick the different spins. Defenders can, however, be vulnerable to topspin either down the middle or wide to the forehand. If the looper waits for the right ball, especially the ball that stands up a little in the middle of the table and topspins it quickly down the middle, it can be very effective. It can also find gaps wide to the forehand, but most players seem to get into position easier to the backhand.

For a defender to survive against the sort of attacking treatment he gets today it is absolutely essential he defends with variety. Otherwise he becomes merely a retriever, which rarely succeeds. If you have ever seen Norio Takashima, the Japanese player who has been one of the world's best choppers, you will know he never just retrieves but varies the spin on almost every shot. He also

knows exactly what he has put on the ball. A retriever will have to take chances in counter-attack because his defence may not be good enough for him to sit back and wait to win the rally. Takashima has no such problems. He continues patiently until he forces the opponent to make a mistake or put the ball too high.

This brings us to the final ingredient essential for a defender to have any chance today. He must have the flats – the flat kills to take advantage when the attacker is forced to push, and pushes too high. Having broken the game up he must then be able to attack suddenly, backhand or forehand, and give the aggressor a sudden, dramatic taste of his own medicine.

Chapter 13
The Lob

Another good method of defending is using an exaggerated loop, away from the table. Around this shot it is possible to base a whole style of play, slowing the play down with topspin from a distance and then speeding it up again. In these circumstances the line between defence and attack is often small.

When this shot is really exaggerated it becomes a lob. This happens when the defender is forced a long way from the table and throws the ball really high to create a chance of recovering (see pictures 33 and 34). The topspin is crucial. To the spectator it may look as though the lobber is in a hopeless position, and is defending in this way as a last resort, but that is not necessarily so. The topspin lob gives it unpredictability. It will shoot. Good lobbers really throw it high, hit the ball solidly, and use wrist spin at the last second. It can be hard to beat.

Take Jacques Secretin of France or Dragutin Surbek of Yugoslavia. Both lob brilliantly with so much topspin that it kicks viciously and is much more difficult to smash than an ordinary lob. This shot is now used very effectively by many of the best players in the world. It is hard work for an opponent who has played a lot of quick rallies, often hard rallies, and then has to smash five, six, seven, eight balls. He can become very tired. For this reason the lob can be used quite deliberately and not just as a last line of defence.

The situation is usually about 70–30 in favour of the attacker winning any particular point in a lob–smash rally – but winning that particular point may not be the important thing. Indeed that may be the effect during the succeeding points when the opponent is tiring. A top player sometimes accepts he will not win the rally, provided he does not lose it

71

too easily. When he eventually does win a rally by lobbing the opponent may easily become uptight, and in the next rally may try to win the point too quickly. He may rush the shot when smashing. So clever players sometimes lob in order to alter the mental state of an opponent. Secretin and Surbek have been masters of that, and have even been cheeky enough to start matches this way. But for most players the lob is just a useful option to have in the locker.

Chapter 14
The Flick

The conventional return against a short serve is a push, a little touched push just over the net. Although this is safe it can create a safety-first attitude. Learning to commit yourself mentally is a large part of being able to attack successfully, and that is the whole point of attempting to flick the return of service.

To attempt it you need to be able to read the service correctly. You need to be aware of when a server is chopping the ball, what contact he has made and exactly what spin is coming over the net at you. You should know that if he plays the ball on the top of his bat, the ball is floated. Things have to be just right with the flick because the margin for error is not great. Read it wrong and you lose the point immediately.

You will only succeed if you take the flick right at the top of the bounce. It has to be done very quickly, and the secret is to come in with the bat nearly horizontal, almost underneath the ball, as though you were going to push (see picture 35), and then turn it over at the very last split second (picture 36). You disguise it with the wrist action. If you were to approach with the bat vertical the opponent would have a good idea of what you were going to do. Also, it would not create the same turning over of the bat, which is very important against a ball with backspin.

The full flick, turning the bat over nearly 180 degrees (see picture 37), gives power, which can be needed to knock the spin off the ball. Obviously if there is no spin on the ball you don't need to use this complete turn-over, or to get underneath the ball. It is then safer to come in with the bat more vertical, although the opponent may be able to read what you are going to do.

35

36

37

Use disguise

You can often make an outright winner with the flick, although it is risky. The ideal is to aim for deception. If the opponent is waiting for the flick, or has read it correctly and has got in position, there can be difficulties. Then, although it may have been a good return, the receiver will be stuck over the table – and if the server follows up well there won't be time to recover. Therefore a technique is needed that enables a player to strike the ball well and also helps to create disguise.

If you are a combination-bat player and use the anti-loop rubber it may not be necessary to come in underneath the ball. But to come in like that with reversed rubber against a chopped ball would cause it to drop off the bat.

An aggressive forehand topspin player will use the flick return quite a lot. He will want to return serve with the forehand no matter where the ball is, and will stand in the backhand corner ready to do so. The flick also stops the opponent following up with his attack.

Some players can flick off both backhand and forehand and this is very valuable. It helps to break up the little touch-touch situations that sometimes occur. Even more valuable, the development of table tennis suggests that the player who flicks first will be at an advantage in future. After the flick the ball still has backspin on it, so the opponent tends to have to lift it up. This enables the player who flicks first to get in position to do an aggressive topspin against lifted topspin – a successful loop the loop.

Chapter 15
The Drop Shot

There are two types of drop shot. One is against a chopped ball and is played with the bat underneath the ball (picture 39), the other (picture 38) is played with the bat over the ball against a topspin.

The first is a little like the touch shot players use to return the ball close to the net to keep the attacker out. This is shown in picture 39. It is played this way against a chopped ball. If a drop shot is tried against a floated ball it will probably go back too high because there is no spin on it. Your opponent will then come back in and smash it past you. This drop shot is best used, therefore, against a very heavily chopped return that lands as a mid-table ball. If it is a good length and low it is very difficult to play a drop shot.

A drop shot is sometimes better played with the forehand because with the backhand you have to come under the table with your legs. Putting your right leg in and then bringing it out again is more clumsy and difficult and takes too much time.

Once you have played a drop shot against a defensive player ideally it is best to send him away from the table again. That will require a fast top-spin. But against combination-bat players this is sometimes easier said than done. These players want the opponent to push because they will often win pushing rallies. There is, though, an important difference between pushing the ball back and drop-shotting it. If you drop-shot properly a defender can't come in and play the pushes, but has to dig the ball up instead.

The other drop shot, as shown in photograph 38, is played when a looper has been forced away from the table, throws the ball up, and returns it short. It is risky to try it against sidespin. It can, though, be used as the finish to a smashing rally after the lobber has been forced into a weaker reply.

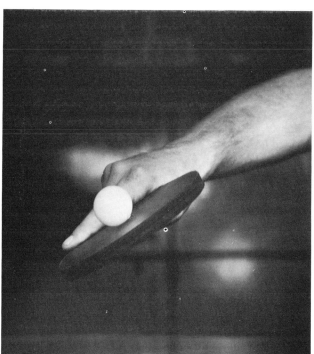

38

39

Chapter 16
Tactics

The first thing that good players think about is not how to play a shot, but where to play it. This is particularly true of combination-bat players but it is important for all players to consider. You should try to assess your opponent – what type of player he is, what he likes to do, where he is likely to put the ball. The game often resembles high-speed chess or cat-and-mouse.

Only certain kinds of players try to succeed by adapting to each different opponent they meet. Others, particularly those who use 'normal' rubbers, and particularly attackers, may want to concentrate on what they themselves are intending to do. This should not lead to a player adopting the attitude of just going on to see what happens. Try to make things happen, which means you must analyse the game.

If you consider what has happened to table tennis in the last few years, you can see the extent to which tactical analysis has been an ongoing process. Once upon a time defenders used to dominate, and later attackers took over as they improved their loops with new fast rubbers. Then players learnt to push and touch the ball short so that the second bounce landed on the table, and the loopers did not have room to make their attack. The flick helped overcome the touch shot. Then there was a phase of counter-hit, counter-hit; then counter-hit on the backhand and smash on the forehand. More recently, the topspin became more highly developed on the backhand, so that a fast attack from both wings became possible. The recipe for the future is likely to be the smash and the fast topspin loop together.

Problems of defending

Through this greater and greater emphasis on attack, defenders have tried to survive – in few numbers – by employing a greater variety of spins and tactics and, sometimes, by using combination bats. The essence of good defending, though, remains much the same. The ball must be kept deep and not too high. A deep return, especially on return of serve, gives the opponent less time, less angle, and less room, so that he is required to move back in order to topspin. If the defender puts it short, the opponent is given the chance to come in hard or to reply with a very short ball.

The defender is better off away from the table where he has more time. His problem is getting there. A poor length on the return of serve, for instance, will cause the opponent to loop hard and possibly prevent him from taking up a defensive position. Attacking players, by contrast, will not want to push long. They will prefer to touch it low over the net because that stops the loop. Short and long are therefore the two areas of the table most used. The mid-table ball is the one to avoid playing.

These days it is hard to survive as a defender unless you can break the game up by attacking on the forehand and backhand. Playing against defenders it is necessary to know where, and from which service, he likes the ball, and whether he can attack or topspin the first ball. Can he smash or do the flat kills? Half the battle is knowing what you will be able to do and what you cannot do. The attacker needs to be able both to topspin and to smash, the topspin to elicit a high return, the smash to put it away. Once a defender knows an attacker cannot smash the ball, life becomes much more comfortable and he can risk putting returns a lot higher. If the defender is a retriever – merely getting the ball back – it may be better for an attacker just to play more carefully against him than against a player who varies the spin. That alone may put him in charge.

When defence is attack

Against a high quality defender, however, you may need to win the points more quickly because if you give him slow balls his variety of spins can be really aggressive. Some would say in this situation that it is the chopper who is really attacking. This kind of opponent must be brought in, then taken out, then brought in, then taken out again. Never let him achieve a pattern. If he gets into a pattern of knowing where the ball is going he may position himself a lot better than an out-and-out retriever. A retriever who just gets the ball back without variation in spin may, though, be a dangerous attacker. If so you have to be careful and keep him away from the table. After the first few points you should be able to size up what kind of defender he is.

It is impossible to legislate for all the situations in which you may find yourself. Tactics are often a matter of instinct, sensing on the spur of the moment what is necessary to win a point. At other times you may be able to plan in advance because you know a particular player. As we said before, no other game is played with such a wide variety of styles and methods so, of course, tactics form a large and complicated part. But remember, no matter how complicated they are, you can rarely win matches without paying attention to tactics.

Chapter 17
Combination Bats and Materials

It may take years to play properly with a combination bat. You can therefore waste much time if you have not first of all developed a good all-round game. Even then you may have to accept defeats while you are developing your methods with the bat. If you are a junior you should not regard results in junior tournaments as too important anyway.

Playing with a combination bat continues to make unusual demands even after a player has become proficient with it. For one thing you have to be much more aware of what your opponent is doing than the player using 'normal' reversed rubbers who will try to impose his own style much more. For another, you have to learn two versions of every shot – one for each rubber – so success requires you to be totally adaptable. You must use both sides of the bat for defence and attack, backhand and forehand.

If you play with pimples on one side and 'normal' on the reverse you may find you are limited in what you can do with the pimples. Your defence may become stronger because you obtain more vicious backspin, but your attack close to the table may not be as effective. If you hit with the 'normal' side you will probably find a length, but if you hit with the slow anti-spin rubber you can vary the length depending on the angle of your bat. When defending, the ball goes back low with anti-spin while the normal tends to give good length. It is probably best to take the ball a yard further back when using the normal. Since the advent of the different colours for different rubbers rule, the effectiveness of slow anti-spin has been limited. But players using it have always been particularly vulnerable to opponents who can read it because slow anti-spin does not provide many alternatives.

81

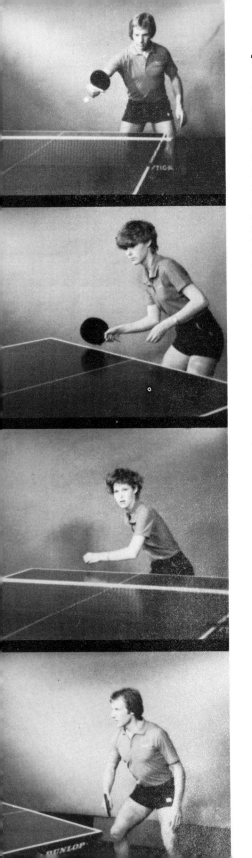

Twiddling

The advantage of anti-spin rubber is that you have control even though you lack the variation. That makes it particularly important to twiddle the bat, using both sides all the time to provide variety in spins and in length. (Remember, though, you can no longer twiddle underneath the table before serving.) If you twiddle during the rally it is best to do so immediately you have played the last shot. Then your opponent may not see what happens because he is watching the ball. Try to twiddle just as his eyes are making contact with the ball, which is usually as it is travelling over the net. Then it is difficult for him to see what you are doing and even lateral vision from the corner of his eye may not be enough. Since the 1984 rule changes the opponent can, though, see clearly which colour rubber is used and may therefore adapt to the twiddle as he sees the next shot make contact with the ball.

The twiddle above the table on service can sometimes still be effective, even though the opponent watches carefully for the different colours. If he is not sure which service and which spin you have used then all sorts of possibilities will follow. He may then play negatively and push the ball back. That allows you to push and you can see whether he reads which rubber was used. This can be the most difficult situation of all for an opponent against a combination-bat player and you may win the point there and then. If so, he is under pressure for the next point, so try the anti-spin (if that is what you have) and look to follow up aggressively, because you will probably be expecting him to push. If he flicks instead and misreads the anti-spin, he may flick it off the end of the table, because there is no backspin. If he pushes it may not be to a good length because there is no spin, and the ball may stand up. Then you can get in with a third ball topspin attack. Two nil up!

Everything is now going well. He cannot afford to push, so he may try to put the ball short. He won't push it long because of the fear of the topspin attack. So he may try to flick to try to stop the topspin. He knows he has got to come at you. You will therefore want to give him another anti-spin. If he reads it and flicks it well he probably won't flick long – more likely a controlled middle-table flick – so you know the ball will stand up a little bit. Then you can hit hard with your backhand into his backhand. You can also twiddle up to the table and use both sides. You can give him an anti-spin attack which is very flat, or twiddle and give him the normal reverse which creates topspin and speed.

Thus you can see that the first two points are crucial, and it is very important to get a lead, because all sorts of possibilities develop from that. Then you have the opponent thinking – are you using normal? Are you using anti-spin? Are you following up with topspin, or are you going to hit a backhand or follow up with a push using anti-spin? He will have plenty to worry about.

The importance of a good start

If those first two points go the way you want, a whole game can sometimes follow successfully from them. Perhaps, therefore, you should start with two widely varied serves – one that is severe with a lot of backspin and one with no spin at all. Serve about fifty-fifty with the anti-spin and with the normal. If that doesn't work, change your tactics.

Next you could stand square to the table and serve short to the middle. This would give no backspin and no float, just a little topspin if anything – a 'nothing' ball played with the bat vertical. That short 'nothing' serve looks easy, but it is tight, and there is often not much that can be done with it. It is difficult to return such a ball short, so the opportunity is there for the server to follow up with topspin. If the receiver comes in and plays a backhand flick he will almost certainly put it down the middle or to the backhand – and then you can play a backhand hit with the opponent over the table.

These tactics with combination bats used to be more effective than they are now, and since the rule changes you can no longer rely on them so much. Combination-bat players sometimes limit themselves to playing with one rubber on one wing – say, long

83

pimples on the backhand for blocking and a fast reversed rubber on the forehand for all-out attack. But a good all-round player who uses the combination of rubbers cleverly can still be a puzzle for an opponent.

Chapter 18
Physical Fitness and Training

The depth of mental strength required to achieve a European title can only be attained by relentless self-punishment over countless hours spent pounding pavements and in gymnasium workouts. Desmond Douglas and Denis Neale have often performed in outstanding fashion for England, yet, up to the time of writing, neither has carried their tremendous team event performances through to the individual events that follow, and won a world or European title.

Table tennis is a more physical game than ever it used to be, and at a high level it requires you to be extremely fit. No longer can you just stand, serve, push and hit. The movements are many, various and strenuous.

It can be a problem to make budding young players realize just how important the physical side is, not only for the movements that are required, but for the mental strength necessary if you are to reach a high standard. If your physical condition is good, then you can get through work in almost any walk of life. That means you can cope with stress more easily as well. There are two essentials in this: the first is longish runs or jogging to build you up, mentally and physically, so you can continue to play for longer periods of time; then there is the sprint work to develop speed.

General fitness is achieved by regular runs. Regular means every morning, even during competition. Perhaps most especially during competition a player needs to get up and just jog for ten minutes to get everything going, to get the stiffness out from the day before. To be able to do that you need to have already done the necessary training. During the season runs should be short so that you do not get weary, but in the summer they should be extended to three or four miles. It is good for stamina. When

there are still two miles to go and it is hurting then it is good for the development of mental strength too. That is the way the Japanese think. A situation will inevitably one day arise in a match when you are under pressure and you really have to knuckle under. The person who has developed the ability to do this is more likely to be the winner.

Strength and suppleness

After this you need stretching exercises, so that your muscles are strong but relaxed. In particular the muscles at the back of the thigh must be supple. This is particularly important for a defensive player because he is bending a lot, a good deal more than an offensive player. Strengthening stomach muscles with sit-ups and leg raises is also valuable. Leg-raises improve the abdominal muscles, strengthen the thighs and help the knees.

Most of the physical training exercises developed over the years are forward movements, but when you analyse table tennis you find that much of the time players are moving backwards, perhaps as much as forty per cent of the time. More thought should be given to backwards and also to sideways movement in training. Training movements should be related to, and reproduce, those made during a game. The Chinese probably do this, although nobody can be certain because they rarely reveal how they train. Shadow play – playing without a ball – perhaps in front of a mirror, can be useful. It is also good to look at what you do. Many players are surprised when they see themselves on video because they did not realize how they moved into a shot.

Flexibility, developed by stretching, is needed to help you open out after a shot. Flexibility permits the shoulders to come round for the big shots, the forehand smash or topspin, and also enables the arm swing to come through quickly. There are plenty of exercises for the upper part of the body. Bounding exercises produces elasticity and strength, and these are so useful they are worth describing.

These are really six exercises in one – hopping on one leg for thirty metres; hopping back on the other leg; then using giant strides, stretching and lifting as much as possible; high knee lifts, lifting the knees as much as possible; then double bunny hops, as they are sometimes called, keeping your legs together all the time and kicking off from both legs; and the last one is sprinting. Five or six sets of these and you will develop, no two ways about it.

How to enjoy it

Enjoyment is vital if you are to train well, and to keep on doing so. Putting people into teams and making them compete can achieve this. There are other exercises which create enjoyment as well. Try the following exercise for developing the ability to get down quickly for a topspin and to recover. Set up a gymnasium box at its lowest level, perhaps two feet off the floor. Stand on the box and drop forward, and immediately do a double knee jump as far forward as possible. Do this six times and then raise the box to about three feet. Again drop, and then go as far forward as possible in a double-legged jump. Do six of those, and then put the full box together, which should measure about four feet six inches high, and do six more. After five minutes' rest start again at the lowest level, but instead of a forward motion go for height. It is long jump and then high jump. You can have a line held up or erected two feet high. When you drop off the top level of the box and try to jump over two or three feet for the first time the effect is almost unbeliev-able – the next day you can't walk. That is because of the muscles you have not used before, muscles you need for table tennis.

It is much harder to train alone. Training with other people will help you do it better, and not to cheat or delude yourself. It can take a long time for players, even those at a high standard, to accept that to be at their best they have to train as much as they practise. Of course it is often difficult to find time to fit everything in. But only those that do so, that go through the shadow play, and the practice on the table, and physical training, will become the really top class players.

Chapter 19
Psychology

We tend to teach a lot about techniques, and even spend a fair amount of time training. We don't, however, talk enough about the mental side of the game. A great deal in table tennis, especially once you are out there competing, is mental. The better you become, the more important it is to get in shape psychologically. You need to prepare yourself psychologically, as well as physically, technically, and tactically. To put it simply, you have to get yourself into the right frame of mind. English players are not always good at this.

Being in good shape physically encourages the right frame of mind. Knowing that you are fit and have done the build up in training often has the effect of building you up in your mind as well. The energy that you accumulate often makes you more aggressive, and for many players that is especially important. A perfect example is the Chinaman Cai Zhen-Hua. In the 1981 World Championship semi-final in Novi Sad his mental state was up to boiling point. Every time he won a point he showed his fist and he ran a circle round his own court. It certainly helped him to win from 4–10 down in the final game against the former world champion from Sweden, Stellan Bengtsson.

Such aggression can be difficult if you have too friendly a relationship with your opponent. A good example of someone who knows this is the tennis player John McEnroe. He does not often socialize off court with other players. You may not want to be quite the same as this, but at the highest level it may sometimes be best to cut yourself off from opponents for a while to get into an aggressive winning frame of mind.

Getting through to the opponent

Another thing you can try that McEnroe does well is to show your opponent just how badly you want to win. That does not mean you should behave like McEnroe when he goes over the top. A good example of how to do it properly is Nigel Eckersley who fights so hard for every point and is so obviously disappointed when he loses one that it can get through to the opponent. You must not let this happen to you. Don't let anything bother you, especially just before or at the beginning of a match, when you most feel unsettled. Before a match there are some players who will go through three, four, or five boxes of balls in order to choose one – even though they are perfectly all right – just to let the opponent know that he has gone to great lengths to be ready.

If you are unsettled, it can make you anxious to win points quickly, or at least to hurry the match up. Especially early in their careers some players are prone to impatience. Try and find a way of getting rid of nervous energy. Extra physical activity may do this, or perhaps deliberately slowing down, or occasionally towelling down. It is important to get to know yourself, and your reactions, and how they affect your play.

You can also try perfectly legal and reasonable psychological ploys. If, for instance, you have lost a point quickly you might just walk up to the table and serve without pausing. The opponent may then play in a more relaxed fashion because he thinks he is on top. That may help you. You might also just serve a quick, small serve to the middle. Then the opponent may respond by not playing as aggressively, returning it more carefully, because he thinks it is a 'nothing' serve.

Nerves can help

Try not to worry too much about being nervous. As you have probably already been told you are more likely to play your best if you are keyed up. Sometimes players, having lost to an opponent, think a little negatively when they meet again.

Because they have lost they think the opponent will be that much more confident. In reality if last time you lost narrowly it is the ideal situation in which to do really well. You ought to be more motivated, and will have had a chance to learn from the previous contest, perhaps more than your opponent has. You could be right in thinking he may be too confident, and possibly less careful than last time.

Remember you cannot be at your best all the time. You will tend to play at or near your peak for a while, but it should not surprise or worry you if your standard goes down again. That is normal. When your schedule is hard you will sometimes go to a tournament or match finding you cannot mentally give one hundred per cent, though you should always try to. If you are to get the best from yourself your preparation needs to take into account how much work and competition you have had. Your life needs to be straightforward too, so that your mind is clear and free of problems other than those of table tennis. If you are preoccupied with arranging travel, or your job, or your private life, or where you have to be next week, you cannot concentrate fully on the match in hand.

Why not win?

Singlemindedness is important. If you have had to take one or two knocks in life it can be turned to your advantage because it can help make you mentally tougher. That may help you to achieve the attitude which says: 'What reason have I for not wanting to beat him?' Try not to be frightened of the consequences of winning as many players are. It is like being a gun-fighter. If a player has beaten good opposition he knows that a lot of opponents are going to be gunning for him. Others are frightened to win because they are going into the unknown. It is the player that is willing to take the chance of getting over the barrier, when it is 19–19, or 20–17, or deuce in the final game, who will win – only those determined not to be frightened will really be successful. There are probably a hundred players in Europe who have enough technique and power to reach the top twenty, but when it comes to the crunch most fall down. Just a few players in England have what it takes. Look at Desmond Douglas: if he has a chance of winning he usually does. Once you develop a negative attitude it is difficult to escape it.

If what you have achieved in life has not been easy you may have an inbuilt necessity to succeed. To do that you need to be psyched-up, yet at the same time enjoying what you are doing. That is why it is often important before going on the table to get away from the match situation, to go out into the corridors at the back and do your mental preparation along with your physical warm-ups. Most players like to be alone and quiet when they do this. When you go to the table you will indeed be alone and it is important to be conscious of nobody, not people watching, not the umpire, nobody. Try not even to be conscious of your opponent, but only his game.

Here and now and no more

If you feel inferior to an opponent you will probably worry about what he is going to do. Instead of doing that try to concentrate on what is actually happening and not what might happen. All you should be concerned about are the ball, the opponent's wrist and his body action. There is no need even to look at his face. If you concentrate on the game, his style of play, and not what he might do, you may find that on the day he does something different from what you have seen or heard about.

Sometimes too much pressure is placed on young players to win. This can affect them adversely. If they have become used to winning at junior level it may be difficult to come through the disappointments needed to become a good senior. The first year out of juniors breaks a lot of players. Coaches should make it clear that it sometimes takes quite a while to develop. You may not necessarily become a good player at seventeen or eighteen, and perhaps not until you are twenty-three or twenty-four or even later. It is important to go on working despite discouraging results.

Too many players play too much for the end result. They don't just want to play for its own sake, and they don't enjoy playing, or enjoy practising enough. Focusing too much on the result can create a barrier. It is always possible to get something out of a match or out of your practices. Enjoy the opportunity to improve – for enjoyment is the most important thing of all. That, after all, is the main reason table tennis exists.